My dads ar embarrassing!

Pablo Fernández

Text and illustrations by Pablo Fernández

© Pablo Fernández 2016

All rights reserved. No part of this book shall be reproduced, stored in a retrieval system, or transmitted by any means electronic, mechanical, photocopying, recording, or otherwise without written permission from the author.

LEGO® is a trademark of the LEGO Group of companies which does not sponsor, authorise or endorse this publication.

Xbox® video game system is a trademark of the Microsoft® corporation which does not sponsor, authorise or endorse this publication.

For my son, the most wonderful boy.

For my family.
I love you to infinity and beyond.

Thank you to Mara, Tita, Jeannie and Carolyn for their useful feedback and suggestions.

Extra special thanks to Rafi, the four-year old literary critic.

My name is Ben. I'm 9 years old and I live with my two dads.

There are good things and bad things about living with my dads. I've made a list.

My dads cook nice things for me, like macaroni cheese, which is my favourite food.

But they also make me eat greens and tomatoes. I HATE tomatoes. Tomatoes are evil!

My dads take me on trips. We discover new places and we do fun things.

But they also take me to boring places like museums (some are OK, but I haven't told my dads that).

My dads got me an Xbox and I love playing with it.

But they limit my time on the Xbox. They go on about screen time and tell me I'll get square eyes!

My dads take me to the cinema and as a treat we have popcorn and fizzy drinks.

But they won't let me see some movies even if my friends have seen them. That's so unfair!

My dads take me camping. We have a great time together.

But they still make me help out. That shouldn't be allowed when you're on holiday!

My dads love the things I build with my Lego.

But they make me clear up the pieces after I'm done!

My dads take me to football training and come to watch my games.

But my dads aren't like other dads...

I never talk about it, although sometimes people notice.

It's SO Embarrassing! Don't tell anyone, but the thing is...

My dads don't like football!

They know NOTHING about football! The teams, the players... I've explained the offside rule a million times and they still don't get it!

Sometimes I wish my dads were like everyone else's dads.

But most of the time...

I love them just the way they are!

To watch videos of how the illustrations for this book were created and find out more about Pablo go to:

www.pablofcreative.com

10% of all proceeds from the sale of this book will benefit New Family Social, a registered charity run by and for LGBT adopters, prospective adopters and foster carers.

To find out more, visit
www.newfamilysocial.org.uk

Printed in Great Britain
by Amazon